MW01616371

Copyright © 2018

Written by Kenneth Perry

Edited by Tiffany N. O'Brien

Photographs by Kenneth Perry unless credited otherwise.

ISBN-10: - 1-946490-20-2

ISBN-13: - 978-1-946490-20-9

DEDICATION

I would like to dedicate this collection of planning guides to two influential people in my life, Joe, and Cindy Perry. My son, Joe Perry, for revitalizing me with the desire to search out and enjoy the beautiful country and its natural resources we have and to explore all of the National Parks; and my lovely wife, Cindy Perry, who supported me in the writing of this planning guide. I am very fortunate to find a unique woman that not only enjoys nature, travel, etc. but is always up for the next adventure.

ABOUT THE AUTHOR

Kenneth is a Certified Interpretive Guide (CIG) through the National Association of Interpretation (NAI) and has visited all of the 50 United States in addition to many European countries, the Caribbean, Mexico, and Canada. Kenneth has visited 34 National Parks and 32 National Monuments. Cindy has visited 31 National Parks, most of which were before their marriage, and are now going to see them together (Ahhh!). As of 2017, there are 59 National Parks and 84 National Monuments. They will be traveling in their motorhome to visit most of the parks, excluding Hawaii and the Virgin Islands. Bailey, their dog, has also been quite the little traveler.

Kenneth started providing trip planning in 2015 to aid travelers in getting the most out of their vacation. The books leverage off of in-depth field experience at each of the National Parks and Monuments. So whether you only have a day, week, or month, you will be provided with the must see and do activities.

The purpose of this planning guide is to provide you with a plethora (always loved that word from the movie "Three Amigos") of information before and during your trip so that you can focus on what you would like to spend your time on during your vacation. If you purchased the paperback, you could also download the eBook either for free or at a very minimal cost.

There are additional pictures posted on the website at NationalParkPlanningGuides.com for each of the parks that did not make it into my books. Feel free to copy and print them, or add them to your vacation slideshow/photos.

National Park Planning Guides Contact Information:
Website: NationalParkPlanningGuides.com
Facebook: www.facebook.com/NationalParkPlanningGuides/
Email: NationalParkPlanningGuidesInfo@gmail.com

HOW TO USE THE PLANNING GUIDE

No matter whether you purchase the ebook or paperback, it will be a great planning resource to bring along on your trip to the national park. However, for some of the larger and more visited parks, I would suggest ordering the book one or more years in advance of the trip as the accommodations at these parks are limited and book up quickly.

The book is designed to eliminate the hours and hours of research for things to do on your vacation. When we used to travel, we would gather all of the brochures that looked interesting along the way. Most of which we just stacked up on a table in the corner of the room. Then we would pick things to do and wing it.

When we got home, we had more of a chance to review some of the information that we picked up. Then we would say, "I wish we would have known that special event was going on; it looks great."

This planning guide will eliminate those things from happening by determining what is important to you to see and do. The ebook is portable on your iPhone, Android, iPad, tablet, or laptop. As you see things of interest, you will have the website, phone number, and description at your fingertips, and you can check them out and also get reviews to help you plan.

This book will help you identify:

- Lodging and Campgrounds in the park
- Campgrounds near the park
- Hiking Trails in the park
- Tours in the park
- Personal Recommendations
- Local Attractions
- Restaurants
- Local area tours

Even though I am focusing my books on the National Parks and National Monuments, there is so much more than the National Park Service provides for us to visit and explore. These include:

National Battlefields (11)   National Battlefields Parks (4)
National Battlefields Site (1) National Military Parks (9)
National Historic Parks (50)   National Historic Sites (78)
International Historic Sites (1) National Lakeshores (4)

National Memorials (30)   National Monuments (84)
National Parks (59)   National Parkways (4)
National Preserves (19)   National Reserves (2)
National Recreation Areas (18)   National Rivers (5)
National Wild and Scenic Rivers and Riverways (10)
National Scenic Trails (3)   National Seashores (10)
Other Designations (11)

Total of 413 as of August 24, 2016

Information on Park Passes:

A summary of park pass options are provided below. For more detailed information, please visit the National Park Service website: https://www.nps.gov/planyourvisit/passes.htm.

4th Grade Pass - This pass is valid for the duration of the 4th grade school year. This free pass for the 4th grader admits the entire family. Here are some of the details about the program.

- Cost: Free (valid for the duration of the 4th grade school year though the following summer (September-August)

- Available for: U.S. 4th graders (including home-schooled and free-choice learners 10 years of age) with a valid Every Kid in a Park paper pass

How to obtain:

- Paper passes can be obtained by visiting the Every Kid in a Park website and can be exchanged for the Annual 4th Grade Pass at federal recreation sites that charge Entrance or Standard Amenity fees (Day Use Fee) (see PDF list of federal recreation sites that issue passes).

- Digital version of the paper pass (such as on smart phones or tablets) will not be accepted to exchange for an Annual 4th Grade Pass.

- More information:

  - Non-transferable.

  - Educators can also be involved! Learn more at the Every Kid in a Park website.

- Additional Details about the Annual 4th Grade Pass (USGS website)

Senior Pass - $80.00; (aka Golden Age or Golden Access Passports) is an interagency lifetime pass that admits the owner and up to three members "that arrive in the same vehicle."

Military Pass - FREE for those while on active duty and includes the owner and up to three members "that arrive in the same vehicle."

Interagency Annual Pass - $80; is an annual pass that admits the owner and up to three members "that arrive in the same vehicle." This pass allows up to two different owners, who must sign the back of the pass.

Permanent disability - FREE and includes the owner and up to three guests "that arrive in the same vehicle."

"A pass is your ticket to more than 2,000 federal recreation sites. Each pass covers entrance fees at national parks and national wildlife refuges as well as standard amenity fees (day use fees) at national forests and grasslands and lands managed by the Bureau of Land Management, Bureau of Reclamation, and U.S. Army Corps of Engineers. A pass covers entrance, standard amenity fees, and day use fees for a driver and all passengers in a personal vehicle at per vehicle fee areas (or up to four adults at sites that charge per person). Children age 15 or under are admitted free."

Since things change frequently, please check the website for updates to the current/future editions for the latest information at NationalParkPlanningGuides.com under the Revisions tab. If you send me your email address, I will email them to you when changes occur. Positive reviews on Amazon are always helpful, and if you have any suggestions or additional information that would be helpful, please leave a comment on my website.

Thank you, and have a great adventure.

CONTENTS

1 CARLSBAD CAVERNS OVERVIEW

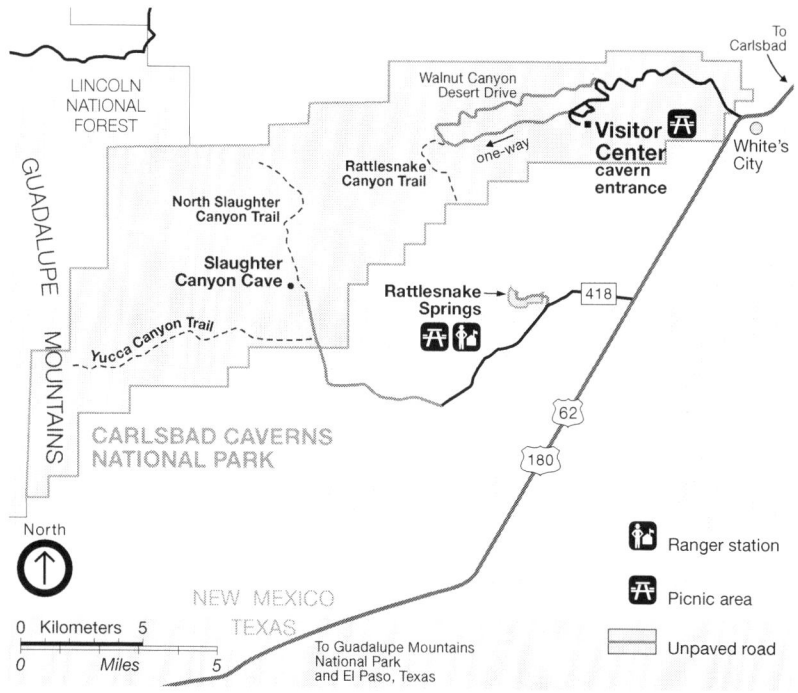

Carlsbad Caverns became a National Monument on October 25, 1923 and a National Park May 14, 1930. The park covers approximately 46,000 acres. It is located in southeastern New Mexico and was visited by 520,026 visitors in 2017.

Contact Information: 3225 National Parks Highway, Carlsbad, NM 88220

Website: https://www.nps.gov/cave/index.htm
Physical Address: 727 Carlsbad Caverns Highway, Carlsbad, NM 88220

Phone number: (575) 785-2232

GPS Coordinates: 32°10'31"N 104°26'38"W

ADA Accessibility: The visitor center is accessible; however, the trails are not recommended due to the terrain variations.

Admission Fee: Cavern Entrance Fee $10 for Adults (16 or older) - $10 Children (15 and under). Ranger-led hikes into the cavern have discounted rates for children. Free entrance when using special passes (see the information on Park Passes section of "How to use the Planning Guide").

Hours: Open every day, except Thanksgiving, Christmas, and New Year's Day. Winter Hours are from Labor Day to the day before Memorial Day 8:00 AM -5:00 PM (The last WALK IN entry is 2:30 PM, and the last Elevator entry to the cave is 3:30 PM). Summer Hours from Memorial Day to the day before Labor Day. The last WALK IN entry is 3:30 PM, and the last Elevator entry to the cave is 35:00 PM. The visitor center winter hours are from 8:00 AM to 5:00 PM, and summer hours are from 8:00 AM to 7:00 PM.

Pet Information: Pets are not permitted in the caverns, however they do have a pet kennel located on the left side of the visitor center. Pets are allowed only in developed areas that include: campgrounds, picnic areas, parking lots, and on the roadways. In those areas they must be on a maximum of a 6 foot leash. They are not permitted on trails or in the back country, and, as always, please clean up after your pet.

Passport Stamp Location: Visitor Center Desk to the left

In addition to the amazing Carlsbad Caverns National Park, it is also part of the Guadalupe Mountains which extend into western Texas. Walnut Canyon Desert Drive is a one way loop near the visitor center that is a must do. Even though the summer temperatures are hot and the winters are cold, the cavern stays at a year-round temperature of 56F (13C). So don't forget to bring something warm before entering the cavern.

Going into commercial caves is kind of like visiting different National Parks in that they are very unique, but generally you will find some special features not found in the rest.

The caverns are home to 17 species of bats, of which 3 species roost in the cavern during late spring through early fall. The largest roosting species is the Brazilian free-tailed with an estimated population of approximately 400,000. Their flights in and out of the cave are from May to October.

There are three other cave locations in Carlsbad National Park:

1. Lechuguilla Cave - 142 miles of caverns with limited access for research and scientific exploration only.
2. Spider Cave - Approximately 5.8 miles of cavern that is undeveloped. Available for ranger-led tours.
3. Slaughter Canyon Cave - Approximately 3.7 miles of cavern that is minimally developed. Available for ranger-led tours.

Early spring is when the desert flowers start blooming on plants, scrubs, and cacti.

The closest town to Carlsbad Caverns is the town of Carlsbad, NM. After driving to the area with miles and miles of desert and mountains you will find the town of Carlsbad. It reminds me of a typical town that may have been on the original US Highway 66 even though it wasn't.

Adequate hotels, restaurants, and RV Camping can be found in the nearby town of Carlsbad.

If you want to experience the bats flying into and out of the cave, they are only there during May-October. Otherwise, any time of the year is a good time to visit the Carlsbad Caverns.

Here is the map with driving distances provided by the NPS. It gives you a good perspective of both National Parks.

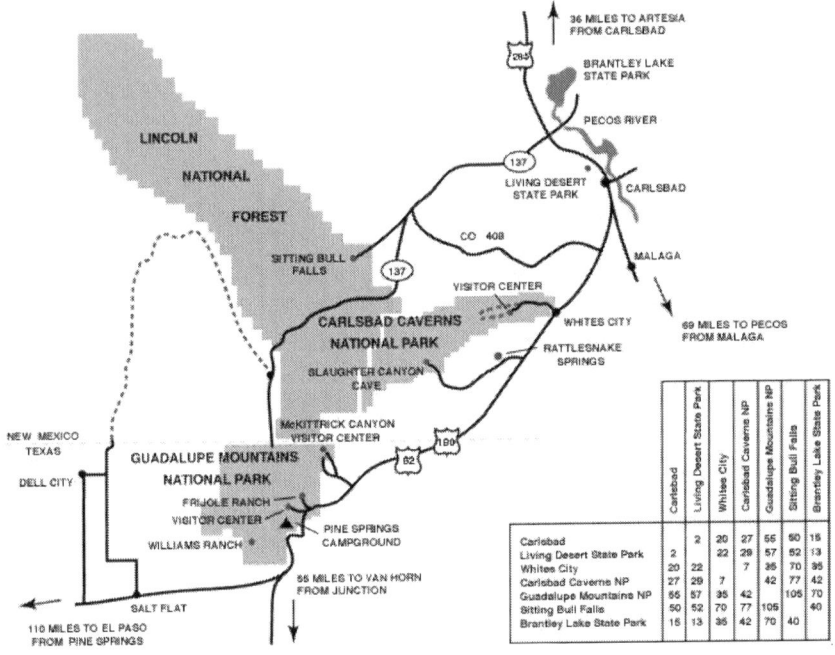

	Carlsbad	Living Desert State Park	Whites City	Carlsbad Caverns NP	Guadalupe Mountains NP	Sitting Bull Falls	Brantley Lake State Park
Carlsbad		2	20	27	55	50	15
Living Desert State Park	2		22	29	57	52	13
Whites City	20	22		7	35	70	35
Carlsbad Caverns NP	27	29	7		42	77	42
Guadalupe Mountains NP	55	57	35	42		105	70
Sitting Bull Falls	50	52	70	77	105		40
Brantley Lake State Park	15	13	35	42	70	40	

Temperatures for the Carlsbad area: Source Weather.com

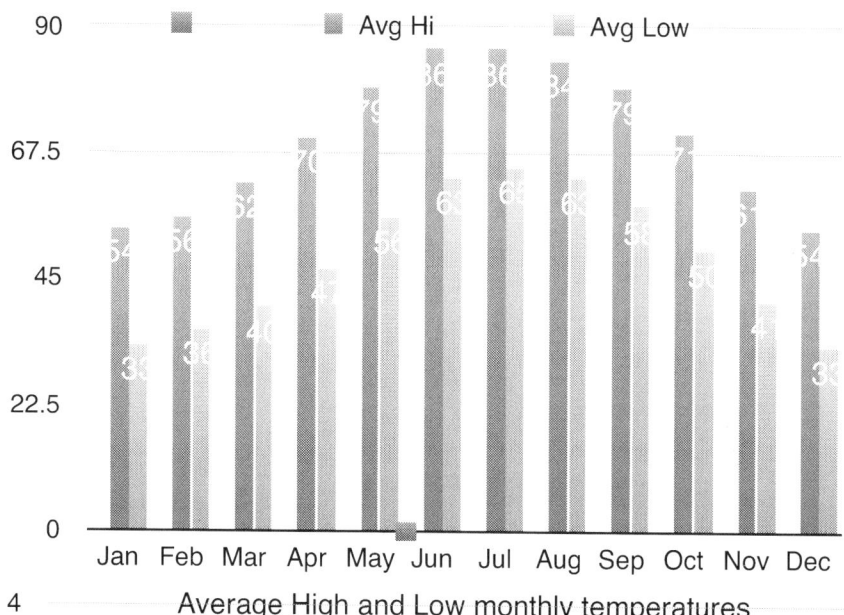

Average High and Low monthly temperatures

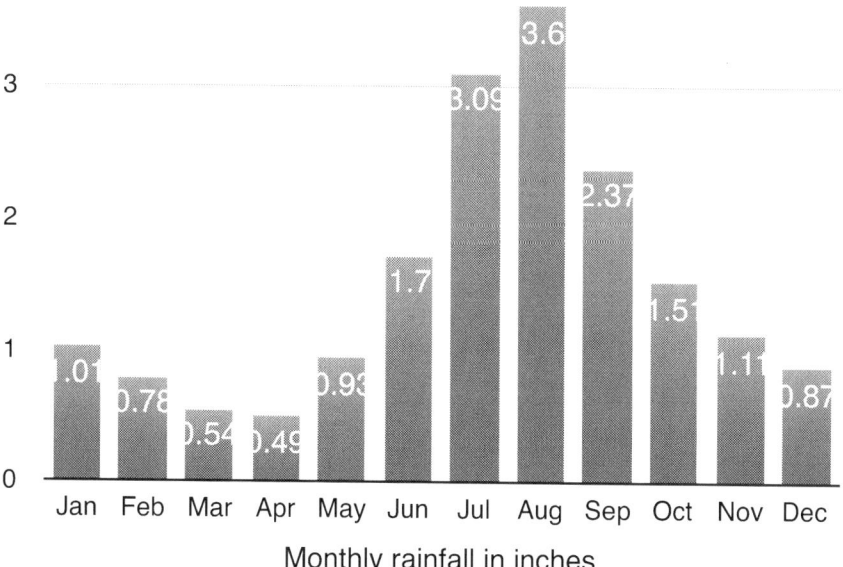

Monthly rainfall in inches

2 CARLSBAD CAVERNS HISTORY

Carlsbad Caverns began approximately 250 million years ago and was an inland reef. Then with the shifting of the earth's surface and uplift, the caverns today are just above the ground water level. The formations that you will see in the cavern are the results of million and millions of years of change eroding the rocks into the beautiful caverns that we have today. Even today the caverns are still changing. The changes are so small that in our lifetime we probably won't see the differences. These changes, like the introduction of petroleum (which was a natural occurrence), in the water created sulfuric acid which dissolved the limestone and created the caverns. Water also deposited minerals onto the formations creating stalactites from the ceiling and stalagmites that developed upward from the cave floor. You will also see things along your travels that look like columns, soda straws, draperies, and popcorn.

Jim White was the first documented explorer of what is now the Carlsbad Caverns. During his exploration of the cavern he named many of the 23 named rooms that exists today which include the Big Room, Green Lake Room, Kings Palace, New Mexico Room, Papoose Room, and Queens Chamber. He also named formations based on his visualization of what they looked like, and some of those were the Fairyland, Giant Dome, Iceberg Rock, Totem Pole, and Witch's Finger.

Mining of guano (bat excrement, used for fertilizer) started 1903. When the National Park was created in 1932, commercial mining was allowed to continue by the National Park Service until 1954. After that, mining has no longer been allowed at Carlsbad Caverns National Park.
Prior to the National Park, visitors had to enter the cave through the natural entrance and walk down the switchback path that took visitors down approximately 750 feet, 230m below the desert floor, and then hike back out on the same path. In 1932 when the NPS took over the day to day operations, they installed an elevator.

In 1955 a second larger capacity elevator was added, and the smaller was retained as a secondary elevator.

In 1978 33,125 acres of Carlsbad Cavern National Park were set aside as wilderness.

After becoming one of the most popular caverns in the world, in 1995 Carlsbad Caverns became a World Heritage Site by United Nations Educational, Scientific, and Cultural Organization (UNESCO).

3 CARLSBAD CAVERNS ACTIVITIES

The most interesting part of going to Carlsbad Caverns is doing the caving tours. You can either do a self-guided tour for free or take one of the Ranger-guided tours for an additional fee. The two must-see areas include the Big Room, which is the largest chamber in North America. The second area is the Natural Entrance, which is a self-guided tour that descends down approximately 750 feet in 1.25 miles to the bottom levels of the cavern.

For those that want to do "real caving", or spelunking as it is known, you'll need to bring old clothes that will get dirty while crawling through the caverns. The rangers provide any safety equipment that you may need, but in some cases you may need to bring some extra items (see table below) for you specific tour.

This is what you may look like on one of the Ranger-led tours.

Carlsbad Ranger-led cave tours

Be sure and check times as they vary based on time of year

Tour	Cost	What will we see?	Notes
King's Palace	$8 for adults, $4 for children, under 4 not permitted. Must also purchase entrance ticket. $4 for Senior and Access Pass holders.	Helictities, draperies, columns and soda straws.	1, 2, 5
Left Hand Tunnel	$7 for adults, $3.50 for children, under 6 not permitted. Must also purchase entrance ticket. $3.50 for Senior and Access Pass holders.	Using historic candle lit lanterns.	1, 3, 5
Slaughter Canyon Cave	$15 for adults, $7.50 for children, under 8 not permitted. $7.50 for Senior and Access Pass holders.	The three major formations are called the Christmas Tree, the Monarch, and the Mushroom.	1, 2, 5, 6
Lower Cave	$20 for adults, $10 for children, under 12 not permitted. Must also purchase entrance ticket. $10 for Senior and Access Pass holders.	You will get dirty... You will visit The Rookery, Colonel Boles Formation, and other formations along your journey.	1, 4, 5, 6, 8
Hall of the White Giant	$20 for adults, $10 for children, under 12 not permitted. Must also purchase entrance ticket. $10 for Senior and Access Pass holders.	You will get dirty...	1, 4, 5, 6, 8, 9
Spider Cave	$20 for adults, $10 for children, under 12 not permitted. $10 for Senior and Access Pass holders.	You will get dirty... Is a three-dimensional maze cave. There you will travel through the Mace Room, Medusa Room, and Cactus Spring room.	1, 4, 5, 7, 8, 9

Source: NPS
Notes:
1. No discounts for Senior and Access Pass holders.
2. Children under 4 not permitted.
3. Children under 6 not permitted.
4. Children under 12 not permitted.
5. Anyone under 16 must be accompanied by an adult
6. Three (3) AA batteries and sturdy hiking shoes or closed-toed shoes.
7. Sturdy hiking shoes or sneakers, drinking water, sunscreen, and a hat are recommended. Walking sticks are allowed on the hiking trail but are NOT permitted inside the cave.
8. NPS will provide helmets with lights, knee and elbow pads, and gloves.
9. This tour may be offered later in 2018?

Kings Palace tour is a 1.5 hour ranger-led hike and will start at 750 feet below the surface and descend down to approximately 830 feet. Once inside the cave it will require descending down approximately 80 feet, and at the end requires walking up a "very steep hill".

Left Hand Tunnel tour is a 2 hour ranger-led activity. Having careful footing is required to navigate steep slippery slopes. Sturdy closed-toed shoes or hiking boots are required, and no backpacks are allowed. Tour starts from the visitor center theater.

Slaughter Canyon Cave tour is a 5.5 hour ranger-led activity. The trails are narrow, uneven, and slippery. Tour starts from the visitor center theater.

Spider Cave tour is a 4 hour ranger-led activity that you will be on your hands and knees crawling through narrow openings. You don't need to be an experienced caver to enjoy this adventure. Tour starts from the visitor center theater.

Lower Cave tour is a 3 hour ranger-led activity that "is a descent of sixty feet of ladders and a knotted rope to hang onto as you slowly walk backward down a slope at the tour entrance". (Source: NPS Lower Cave Tour description) Tour starts from the visitor center theater.

Hall of the White Giant tour is a 4 hour ranger-led activity that has tight, narrow passages and is not recommended of anyone afraid of tight spaces or heights. Two of the areas that you explore include: Matlock's Pinch and the White Giant. Tour starts from the visitor center theater.

Carlsbad Self-Guided Tours

There are two self-guided tours that are free: the Big Room and the Natural Entrance. If you are planning to take this type of tour I recommend that you spend some time at the visitor center and look through the information regarding the formations and what they look like. In the Big Room there are storyboards that provide information, and when we visited, a ranger was near where the Natural Entrance trail enters the Big Room, answering questions.

Big Room Info and Map: https://www.nps.gov/cave/planyourvisit/upload/Accessibility.pdf

I recommend either printing it before you go or download it to your phone for reference.

Big Room is ADA accessible

Natural Entrance - If your hiking ability is like mine, it is much easier going down than climbing up a mountain. The Park Service rates it as 'Strenuous', but I did not have any trouble. Most of the downhill is just a series of switchbacks that didn't seem that steep. However, if I tried to go back up the 750 ft, well that would have been a different story.

The Natural Entrance is included with the entrance fee. See the desk to get the ticket, then proceed to the entrance. As you enter the entrance you may hear and see small birds entering and exiting overhead. As you walk down the path you will see formations that few will get to see.

Once you reach the lower level you will then have access to the truly amazing rooms, all of which are pretty much level ground and mostly ADA accessible. After exploring all of the rooms at the lower level and visiting the cafe and gift shop, you can take the elevator back to the top at no charge. Remember the times for the last elevator going up, see Notes 1 and 2 below.

Tour	Enter the cave	Notes
Big Room	Winter 8:30 AM-3:30 PM Summer 8:30 AM-5:00 PM	1, 2, 3
Natural Entrance	Winter 8:30 AM-2:30 PM Summer 8:30 AM-4:00 PM	1, 2, 3

NOTES:
1. Elevator winter schedule - The last one up at 4:30 PM
2. Elevator summer schedule - The last one up is at 6:30 PM
3. Reminder that exiting the cave via the natural entrance is VERY strenuous. See elevator times.

Carlsbad Bat Flight Program

A FREE program put on by NPS from May-October in the evening at the amphitheater near the mouth of the natural entrance to the cave. The program times are posted and vary depending on the time of sunset. If you are an early riser, stop by and watch the bats re-enter the cave in the morning...

Note: While watching the bats leave or reenter the cave, NPS requests that you do not use an electronic device such as cameras, laptops, cell phones, tables, or MP3 players to protect the bats, as they are very sensitive to sound and lights.

Carlsbad Night Sky Program

A FREE program put on by NPS from May-October in the evening.

Carlsbad Walnut Canyon Desert Drive Loop

Take a short drive from the visitor center to not only get to see some of the park, where you will also join the Rattlesnake Canyon Trail Head if you want to take a hike.

Carlsbad Caverns Hiking

Name	Diff	Trail
Chihuahuan Desert Nature Trail	ADA	mostly paved, 1/2 mile (1 km) loop, 1/2 hour
Old Guano Road	E	3.7 mi (6 km) and 2 hrs one way, elevation change: 710 ft (216 m)
Juniper RIdge	E	3.5 mi (5 km) and 2 1/2 hrs one way, elevation change: 800 ft (240 m)
Rattlesnake Canyon	M	3 mi (4.8 km) and 3 hrs one way, elevation change: 600 ft (183 m)
Upper Rattlesnake Canyon to Guadalupe Ridge Loop	M	6 mi (9.6 km) round trip, 4 hours to complete loop, elevation change: 670 ft (204 m) – map highly recommended
Guadalupe Ridge Loop	D	12 mi (19 km) one way, over night recommended for entire length and return, elevation change ascend: 2,050 ft (625 m)
Slaughter Canyon	D	5.3 mi (8.6 km) one way from parking lot to intersection with Guadalupe Ridge Road, elevation change to ridge top: 1850 (564 m)
Yucca Canyon	D	7.7 mi (12.4 km) one way, elevation change: 1520 ft (464 m)

ADA= ADA accessible, E=Easy, M=Moderate, D=Difficult

Source: https://www.nps.gov/cave/planyourvisit/upload/backcountry_use.pdf

Other activities nearby

Living Desert Zoo & Gardens State Park

Website: http://www.emnrd.state.nm.us/SPD/livingdesertstatepark.html

Phone: (575) 887-5516

Open year round, and is located just north of Carlsbad, NM on US Highway 285.

This native wildlife zoo, accredited by the Association of Zoos and Aquariums, exhibits more than 40 species of animals and hundreds of species of plants native to the Chihuahuan Desert. The park provides an up-close experience for visitors with a variety of fun interpretive programs for every season geared for the entire family. Living Desert also has beautiful hiking trails, picnic areas, and group facilities. There is no camping and no pets are allowed.

Source: Living Desert Zoo & Gardens State Park

Lincoln National Forest (Guadalupe District)

Website: www.fs.usda.gov/lincoln/home

Phone: (575) 885-4181

The 1,103,441 acres is available for hiking, caving, camping, picnicking, horseback riding, hunting, and sightseeing. The Guadalupe Ranger District Office is located at 5203 Buena Vista Drive Carlsbad, NM 88220

Brantley Lake State Park

Website: www.emnrd.state.nm.us/SPD/brantleylakestatepark.html

Phone: (575) 457-2384

4 CARLSBAD CAVERNS PERSONAL FAVORITES

The most interesting part of going to Carlsbad Caverns is doing the caving tours. You can either do a self-guided tour for free or take one of the Ranger-guided tours.

1. We really enjoyed the FREE Natural Entrance self-guided tour. At the booking desk in the visitor center, they will remind you again and again that it is strenuous. You will see signs along the way telling you the same, and just before you get to the cave entrance you will be greeted by a Ranger telling you that it is strenuous and to not touch any of the formations. I found it to be moderate and that is only because of the decline. The few switch backs leading down from the amphitheater will give you an idea of the steepness down to the Big Room; you can turn around here if you would rather take the elevator down. Once at the entrance to the Big Room, it is pretty flat, most of which is ADA accessible. One of the most interesting was the 200,000 ton "Iceberg Rock" that fell from the ceiling. The elevator ride to the top is free, and in no way would I try to ascend out of the cave, because that would definitely be Strenuous. We were there in mid-April and the bats had not come back to the cave. However, we did see small birds entering and exiting the cave at high rates of speed. Here is what the switch backs look like.

Going into the cave through the natural entrance, we were amazed at the amount of small birds that flew in and out of the cave entrance. As we journeyed down into the cave, we were hoping to catch a glimpse of a bat hanging from the ceiling, but we never saw one, but we saw other cool things.

2. While exploring the cave you will find the lighting to be soft, but in most cases I found that the photograph without using a flash worked better. We also found a small stream with a green copper look

3. If you want to experience how true caving is done, bring some old clothes and take one of the Ranger-Led Tours. Some of those caving tours include Spider Cave, Lower Cave, and Hall of the White Giant. The rangers talk about the particulars of the tour, explain your equipment, and describe what you see. After the tour introduction, you will go to an equipment room for your kneepads, elbow pads, harness, and gloves (depending on the level you want to do).

4..The Bat Flight Program is truly amazing to watch hundreds of thousands of Brazilian Free-tailed bats fly out of the cave at sunset or into the cave at sunrise; and yes, you will be safe in the amphitheater seats as the bats fly overhead, silhouetted against the sky.

5. Take a ride on the Carlsbad Walnut Canyon Desert Loop. It is a well maintained dirt road taking you on a scenic ride through the desert.

6. There is a short nature trail that is a 1/2 mile loop for a view of the desert.

5 CARLSBAD CAVERNS ACCOMMODATIONS

Backcountry Camping

There is no camping with RVs or trailers at Carlsbad Caverns National Park; however, backcountry camping is allowed by permit only. Information on backcountry camping can be found on the NPS website at:

https://www.nps.gov/cave/planyourvisit/backcountrypermits.htm

Most National Parks have designated campgrounds and a fixed number of established sites. Carlsbad, however, allows you to pick your own site with the restrictions found in the above website. I really like this style better. And when you leave, remember the next person should never know that you were there...

Local Campgrounds

Name	Phone (575)	Address	Website
Brantley State Park	457-2384	33 East Brantley Lake Rd. Carlsbad, NM	www.emnrd.state.nm.us/SPD/brantleylakestatepark.html
Carlsbad RV Park & Campground	885-6333	4301 National Parks Hwy, Carlsbad, NM	http://carlsbadrvpark.com
Pecos River RV Park	887-9835	320 E Greene St, Carlsbad, NM	https://www.facebook.com/pecosriverrvpark/
Carlsbad KOA Holiday	457-2000	2 Manthei Rd, Carlsbad	http://koa.com/campgrounds/carlsbad/
Windmill RV Park	887-1387	3624 National Parks Hwy, Carlsbad, NM	https://www.facebook.com/.../Windmill-RV-Park/111833755520629

Name	Phone (575)	Address	Website
Whites City RV Park	785-2291	17 Carlsbad Cavern Hwy, Whites City, NM	https://www.facebook.com/WhitesCityNM
Eldorado Estates Mobile Home and RV Park	887-3111	3022 National Parks Hwy, Carlsbad, NM	http://www.eldoradoestates.net
Sun West Mobile City	885-1900	4219 Boyd Dr, Carlsbad, NM	http://www.bcsrealty-sunwestmobilecity.com/RV-Park.html

Lodges and Hotels in the park

There are no lodges or hotels in the park.

Local Lodges and Hotels

Listed below are the main cities near the National Park and the lodging options:

Name	Phone (575)	Address	Website
Rodeway Inn	785-2296	6 Carlsbad Caverns Highway, Whites City	https://www.choicehotels.com/rodeway-inn
La Quinta Inn & Suites	236-1010	4020 National Parks Highway, Carlsbad	http://www.laquintacarlsbadnm.com/?cid=local_google_6628
Sleep Inn & Suites	941-2300	3825 National Parks Highway, Carlsbad	https://www.choicehotels.com/new-mexico/carlsbad/sleep-inn-hotels/nm211?source=gyxt
Days Inn	887-7800	3910 National Parks Highway, Carlsbad	https://www.wyndhamhotels.com/days-inn/carlsbad-new-mexico/days-inn-carlsbad/overview?CID=LC:DI:20160927:RIO:Local:SM-dimotn

Name	Phone (575)	Address	Website
Candlewood Suites South	941-3711	3711 San Jose Blvd, Carlsbad	https://www.ihg.com/candlewood/hotels/us/en/carlsbad/cnmcw/hoteldetail?cm_mmc=GoogleMaps-_-CW-_-USA-_-CNMCW
Fairfield Inn & Suites	887-8000	2525 South Canal Street, Carlsbad	http://www.marriott.com/hotels/travel/cnmfi-fairfield-inn-and-suites-carlsbad/?scid=bb1a189a-fec3-4d19-a255-54ba596febe2
TownePlace Suites	689-8850	311 Pompa Street, Carlsbad	http://www.marriott.com/hotels/travel/cnmts-towneplace-suites-carlsbad/?scid=bb1a189a-fec3-4d19-a255-54ba596febe2
Best Western Stevens Inn	887-2851	1829 S Canal St, Carlsbad	https://www.bestwestern.com/content/best-western/en_US/notice/hotel-not-found.html
Hampton Inn & Suites	725-5700	120 Esperanza Circle, Carlsbad	http://hamptoninn3.hilton.com/en/hotels/new-mexico/hampton-inn-and-suites-carlsbad-CNMNMHX/index.html
Holiday Inn Express	234-1252	2210 West Pierce Street, Carlsbad	http://hiexpresscarlsbad.com
Motel 6	885-0011	3824 National Parks Hwy, Carlsbad	http://www.motel6carlsbad.com

6 CARLSBAD CAVERNS RESTAURANTS

Websites I use for doing a quick check on restaurants and ratings are listed below:

> https://www.tripadvisor.com/Restaurants
> www.foodandwine.com/restaurants
> https://www.zagat.com
> https://www.yelp.com/

Inside Carlsbad Park

Name	Phone (575)	Address	Website
Carlsbad Caverns Trading Company	785-2281	727 Carlsbad Cavern Hwy, Carlsbad	http:// www.carlsbadcavernstradingco. com
Snack bar in the caverns	785-2281	727 Carlsbad Cavern Hwy, Carlsbad	http:// www.carlsbadcavernstradingco. com

White City (outside the park)

Name	Phone (575)	Address	Website
Velvet Garter Saloon and Restaurant	785-2291	26 Carlsbad Cavern Hwy, Whites City	None

Carlsbad, NM (approximately 15 miles from the park)

A= American, B= Bar-B-Que, C= Chinese, D= Diner, G= Grill, H= Hotel, I= Italian, M=Mexican

Name	Type	Phone (575)	Address	Website
Trinity Hotel & Restaurant	H	234-9891	201 S Canal St, Carlsbad	http:// www.thetrinityhotel.com

Name	Type	Phone (575)	Address	Website
Blue House Bakery & Cafe		628-0555	609 N Canyon St, Carlsbad	https://m.facebook.com/BlueHouseBakeryAndCafe/
Happy's	A	887-8489	4103 National Parks Hwy, Carlsbad	None
Chili's Grill & Bar	G	628-1275	2249 S Canal St, Carlsbad	https://www.chilis.com/menu
Danny's Place	B	885-8739	902 S Canal St, Carlsbad	None
IHOP	A	234-1599	2529 S Canal St, Carlsbad	https://restaurants.ihop.com/nm/carlsbad/3362/
Junior's Restaurant	A	725-5465	403 E Greene St, Carlsbad	None
Lucy's Mexicali Restaurant	M	887-7714	710 S Canal St, Carlsbad	https://www.facebook.com/LucysRestaurant/
Larez Restaurant	A	885-5113	1524 S Canal St, Carlsbad	None
Lucy Bull Grill	G	725-5444	220 W Fox St, Carlsbad	http://www.luckybullgrill.com
Becky's Drive In Restaurant	D	885-3262	901 W Church St, Carlsbad	None
Church Street Grill	A	885-3074	301 W Church St, Carlsbad	http://www.churchstreetgrill.com
Dragon China Buffet	C	887-1818	2125 S Canal St, Carlsbad	None
My Daddy's Bar-B-Que	B	628-0196	704 W Pierce St, Carlsbad	None

Name	Type	Phone (575)	Address	Website
Denny's	**D**	885-5600	810 W Pierce St, Carlsbad	https://locations.dennys.com/NM/CARLSBAD/246236?utm_source=yext&utm_medium=local-listing&utm_campaign=yext-listing
Little Italy Cafe	**I**	628-0190	1000 S Canyon St, Carlsbad	None
Yellow Brix Restaurant	**A**	941-2749	201 N Canal St, Carlsbad	http://www.yellowbrixrestaurant.com
Red Chimney Bar-B-Q	**B**	885-8744	817 N Canal St, Carlsbad	http://www.redchimneybbq.com

A= American, B= Bar-B-Que, C= Chinese, D= Diner, G= Grill, H= Hotel, I= Italian, M=Mexican

Guadalupe Mountains

Name	Type	Phone (915)	Address	Website
Spanish Angels Cafe	**M**	964-2208	103 Main St, Dell, TX	None

A= American, B= Bar-B-Que, C= Chinese, D= Diner, G= Grill, H= Hotel, I= Italian, M=Mexican

7 GUADALUPE MOUNTAINS OVERVIEW

Guadalupe Mountains became a National Park on September 30, 1972. The park covers approximately 86,367 acres. It is located in western Texas and was visited by 225,257 visitors in 2017.

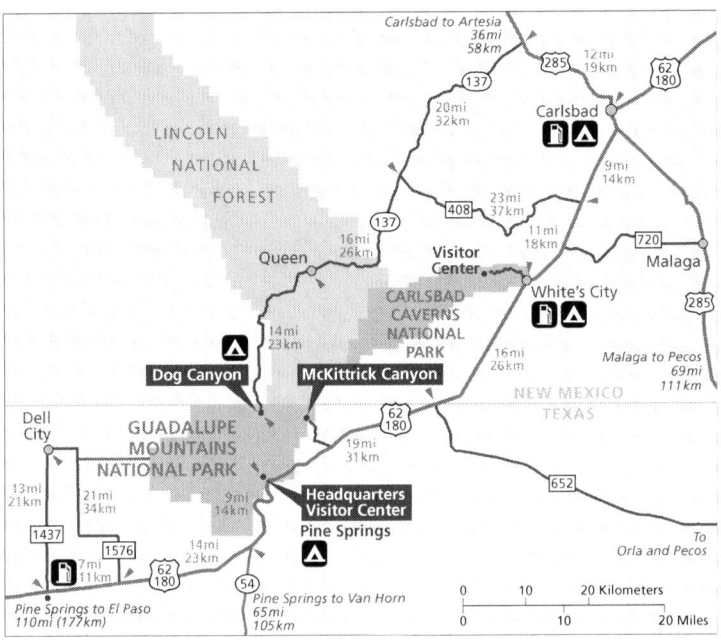

Contact Information: 400 Pine Canyon Salt Flat, TX 79847

Website: https://www.nps.gov/gumo/index.htm

Physical Address: 400 Pine Canyon Salt Flat, TX 79847

Phone number: (915) 828-3251

GPS Coordinates: 31°55'N 104°52'W

ADA Accessibility: The visitor center is accessible; however, the trails are not recommended due to the terrain variations.

Admission Fee: $5 for adults over 16, Children 15 and under free, and $20 annual pass just for the Guadalupe Mountains if you have a pass (see the Information on Park Passes section of "How to use the Planning Guide").

Hours: Open every day, 24 hours a day, except for Christmas day.

Pet Information: Pets are permitted only on the trail between the visitor center and campground and the Pinery Trail. Pets must be kept on a six foot leash. They are allowed only in developed areas that include: campgrounds, picnic areas, parking lots, and on the roadways. They are not permitted on trails or in the back country, and, as always, please clean up after your pet.

Passport Stamp Location: Visitor Center Desk

There are four entrances to the park; east is Dog Canyon, northeast is McKittrick Canyon, southeast is Pine Springs Visitor Center, and from the west on Williams Road from Dell City.

The northeast entrance to Guadalupe Mountains National Park is approximately 20 miles from Carlsbad Cavern National Park. There is only one short road from the northeast entrance that provides access to the Visitor Center from White City. Pine Springs Headquarters and Visitor Center are located on the southeast corner of the park. The park is short on roads; however, offers numerous hiking and backcountry camping opportunities.

The Guadalupe Mountains terrain and landscape varies from the Chihuahuan Desert to beautiful canyons and highlands with 8,000 ft peaks in a magnificent forest with elk, deer, bears and other mammals, birds and others that thrive in this unique wild and protected natural habitat.

Temperatures for the Guadalupe area: Source: weather.com

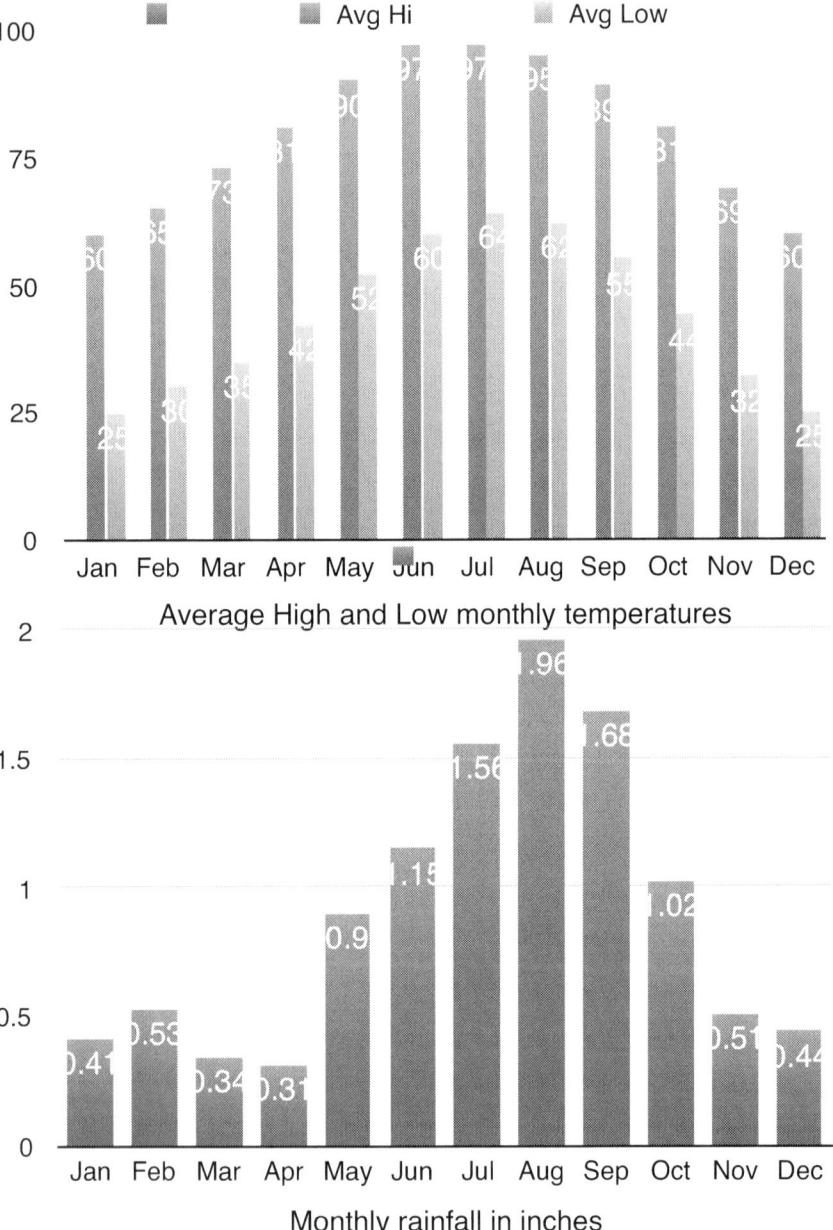

Average High and Low monthly temperatures

Monthly rainfall in inches

Note the temperatures shown above are for the desert. The temperature zone for the high planes can be cooler than the temperatures shown above.

8 GUADALUPE MOUNTAINS HISTORY

The Nde (Mescalero Apache) lived in the Guadalupe Mountains isolated from others until the mid-1800's. As the expansion to the west began in the early 1800's, explorers and pioneers started their migration westward to start a new life. The Nde, unlike some tribes, resisted newcomers from entering their homeland. As a result, conflicts between the Nde and the pioneers resulted in the United States Army in 1849 driving the Nde from their mountain homeland.

The Butterfield Stage line established the first transcontinental mail route that went from St Louis to San Francisco through the Guadalupe Mountains. One of their stops located in the National Park was known as "Pine Spring". There is a monument placed at the entrance to the trail just a short distance from the visitor center with a small pull out.

The trail is short and fairly level. There you can see one wall from the Station and another feature that was probably a storage building.

In the 1920s Wallace E. Pratt, a petroleum geologist, purchased land in the Guadalupe Mountains in McKittrick Canyon. He owned 5,632 acres (23 km²), which he later donated to the National Park Service in 1959. That land includes his former home which is open to the public and a structure that looks like an oil tanker, now a ranger station.

The Frijole Ranch History Museum is located just a short drive from the Pine Springs Visitor Center, east on US 62/180 heading towards Carlsbad. It is a peaceful oasis in the middle of the desert with an interesting underground spring that continually runs within a building and then flows above ground through the property.

Williams Ranch, located in the Shumard Canyon, can be accessed by 4-wheel vehicles with high clearance on the south end of the park. Make sure that you get the key to the gate at the visitor center before you head out… Part of the trip to the ranch will be along the historic Butterfield stage route.

9 GUADALUPE MOUNTAINS ACTIVITIES

There are things to do for everyone here at this national park. They have a website with printable brochures for historical locations, trail guides, geology identification, backcountry, and hiking maps. Here is the link: https://www.nps.gov/gumo/planyourvisit/printable-brochures.htm

Guadalupe Hiking

There is approximately 80 miles of hiking trails, with 10 backcountry campgrounds. Horseback riding is available on 60 percent of the trails.

Name	Diff	Note	Trail	Website for additional information
Guadalupe Peak	S	3	10 miles, 2,906 ft elevation gain, mixed trail	https://www.nps.gov/ gumo/planyourvisit/ upload/ GuadalupePeakTrail.pdf
McKittrick Canyon to Pratt Cabin	M	2	16 miles, 2,700 ft elevation gain, mixed trail	https://www.nps.gov/ gumo/planyourvisit/ upload/ McKittrickDayHikeswithP hotos-2.pdf
Pinery	E	1	.9 miles, 20 Mins, 40 ft elevation gain, paved trail	https://www.nps.gov/ gumo/planyourvisit/ upload/ PineSpringsDayHikes.pdf
Smith Spring	M	1	2.3 miles, 1.5 hours, 402 ft elevation gain, mixed trail	https://www.nps.gov/ gumo/planyourvisit/ upload/ PineSpringsDayHikes.pdf
Devil's Hall	M		3.8 miles, 2.5 hours, 548 ft elevation gain, mixed trail	https://www.nps.gov/ gumo/planyourvisit/ upload/ PineSpringsDayHikes.pdf
Tejas	S		24 miles multi day, 2000+ ft elevation gain, mixed trail	https://www.nps.gov/ gumo/planyourvisit/ upload/TejasTrailmap.pdf
The Bowl	S	3	8.5 miles,	None available

Name	Diff	Note	Trail	Website for additional information
McKittrick Nature Trail	M	1	.9 miles,	None available
El Capitan	M, S	3	11.3 miles,	None available
Frijole & Foothills Trails	M	3	5.5 miles,	None available
Indian Meadow Nature Trail	E	1	.6 miles	None available
Permian Reef Trail	S	3	8.4 miles, 2,000 ft elevation gain,	None available

Notes:
1. Trails are approximately 1 hour hiking time
2. Trails are approximately 2-3 hours hiking time
3. Trails are ONE DAY hikes

Guadalupe Horseback Riding (if you bring your horse)
Horseback riding is available on 60% of the trails. Livestock use is during the day, and horses must return each night to the corrals at either Dog Canyon or Frijole Ranch. Each corral has four pins and will accommodate ten animals. Remember there is no overnight camping on the trails with horses. Park fees for horses can be found on: https://www.nps.gov/gumo/planyourvisit/horse.htm

Reservations may be made by calling (915) 828-3251 ext. 2124 (for Frijole), or (575) 981-2418 (Dog Canyon) between 8:00 AM and 4:30 PM Mountain Time.

Corrals and Camping	Easy Trails	Moderate Trails	Difficult Trails
Dog Canyon	1	3	None
Frijole Ranch	2	4	5

Notes:
1. Foothills Trail
2. Frijole Trail, Williams Ranch Road
3. Dog Canyon to Marcus Trail, Marcus Trail
4. Tejas Trail to McKittrick Ridge Campground, Pine Springs to Salt Basin Overlook
5. Pine Springs to Pine Top, Pine Top to Bush Mountain Campground, Guadalupe Peak Trail and Salt Basin Overlook to Williams Ranch

Guadalupe Bicycling
Mountain bikes and motorized vehicles are prohibited on all park trails.

10 GUADALUPE MOUNTAINS PERSONAL FAVORITES

The Frijole Ranch History Museum is a great place to see. The museum is opened intermittently, but even if it isn't open it is still well worth the visit. It is only a short distance from the main road. While there you can picture how the early settlers were able to make a go of it in the desert. In addition to the old house there is also a schoolhouse, bunkhouse, barn, and livestock area in this little desert oasis.

The "Pinery" where the Butterfield stage stop was is a nice stop; however don't get your hopes up on seeing the complete station. All that is left now is one wall. It is a short walk, and the interpretive signs provide you information into the past history of the line.

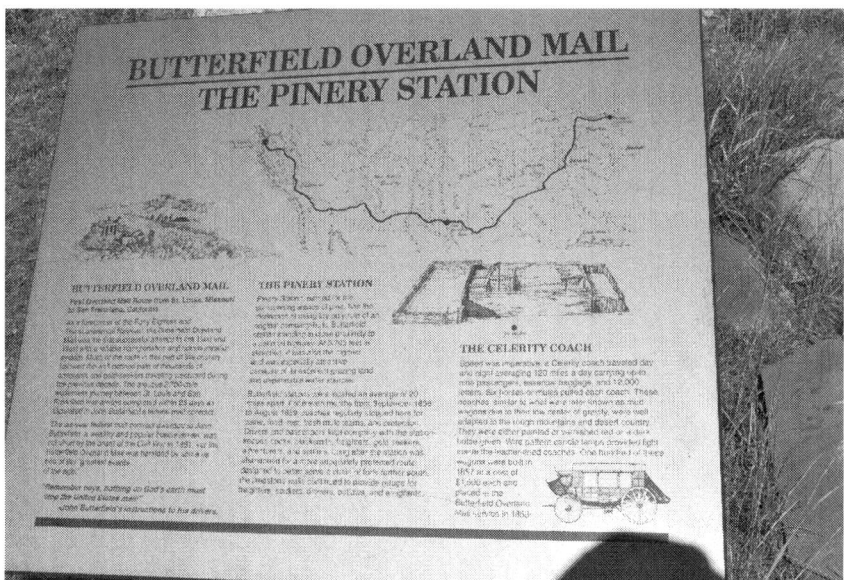

This is a great area to "take a hike" with trails for all abilities. Depending on the hike, you can hike the desert, through canyons, or even in the higher elevations in wooded forests.

11 GUADALUPE MOUNTAINS ACCOMMODATIONS

Hotels near the park
RV/Trailer Camping

The camping for RV's and trailers is first come first serve but usually do not fill up. This is the contact information for the Pine Springs Visitor Center at 915-828-3251.

Campground	Tent Sites	RV Sites	Coral	Group Camping
Pine Springs	20	20	1 (10 horses)	10-20 people (1 site) Reservations
Dog Canyon	9	4	1 (10 horses)	None

Guadalupe Backcountry Campgrounds
Information on backcountry camping can be found on the NPS website at:

https://www.nps.gov/cave/planyourvisit/backcountrypermits.htm

Campground	Sites
Guadalupe Peak	5
Pine Top	8
Tejas	5
Bush Mountain	5
Mescalero	8
McKittrick Ridge	5
Blue Ridge	5

Campground	Sites
Marcus	5
Wilderness Ridge	5
Shumard	5

12 GUADALUPE MOUNTAINS RESTAURANTS

Websites I use for doing a quick check on restaurants and ratings are listed below:

> https://www.tripadvisor.com/Restaurants
> www.foodandwine.com/restaurants
> https://www.zagat.com
> https://www.yelp.com/

Places to eat around Guadalupe Mountains National Park are almost non existent, so I would plan to bring food with you. As a backup Carlsbad is the shortest distance to food.

Inside Carlsbad Park

Name	Phone (575)	Address	Website
Carlsbad Caverns Trading Company	785-2281	727 Carlsbad Cavern Hwy, Carlsbad	http:// www.carlsbadcavernstradingco. com
Snack bar in the caverns	785-2281	727 Carlsbad Cavern Hwy, Carlsbad	http:// www.carlsbadcavernstradingco. com

White City (outside the park)

Name	Phone (575)	Address	Website
Velvet Garter Saloon and Restaurant	785-2291	26 Carlsbad Cavern Hwy, Whites City	None

Carlsbad, NM (approximately 15 miles from the park)
A= American, B= Bar-B-Que, C= Chinese, D= Diner, G= Grill, H= Hotel, I= Italian, M=Mexican

Name	Type	Phone (575)	Address	Website
Trinity Hotel & Restaurant	H	234-9891	201 S Canal St, Carlsbad	http:// www.thetrinityhotel.com
Blue House Bakery & Cafe		628-0555	609 N Canyon St, Carlsbad	https://m.facebook.com/ BlueHouseBakeryAndCa fe/
Happy's	A	887-8489	4103 National Parks Hwy, Carlsbad	None
Chili's Grill & Bar	G	628-1275	2249 S Canal St, Carlsbad	https://www.chilis.com/ menu
Danny's Place	B	885-8739	902 S Canal St, Carlsbad	None
IHOP	A	234-1599	2529 S Canal St, Carlsbad	https:// restaurants.ihop.com/nm/ carlsbad/3362/
Junior's Restaurant	A	725-5465	403 E Greene St, Carlsbad	None
Lucy's Mexicali Restaurant	M	887-7714	710 S Canal St, Carlsbad	https:// www.facebook.com/ LucysRestaurant/
Larez Restaurant	A	885-5113	1524 S Canal St, Carlsbad	None
Lucy Bull Grill	G	725-5444	220 W Fox St, Carlsbad	http:// www.luckybullgrill.com
Becky's Drive In Restaurant	D	885-3262	901 W Church St, Carlsbad	None

Name	Type	Phone (575)	Address	Website
Church Street Grill	A	885-3074	301 W Church St, Carlsbad	http:// www.churchstreetgrill.com
Dragon China Buffet	C	887-1818	2125 S Canal St, Carlsbad	None
My Daddy's Bar-B-Que	B	628-0196	704 W Pierce St, Carlsbad	None
Denny's	D	885-5600	810 W Pierce St, Carlsbad	https:// locations.dennys.com/ NM/CARLSBAD/ 246236? utm_source=yext&utm_ medium=local- listing&utm_campaign=y ext-listing
Little Italy Cafe	I	628-0190	1000 S Canyon St, Carlsbad	None
Yellow Brix Restaurant	A	941-2749	201 N Canal St, Carlsbad	http:// www.yellowbrixrestauran t.com
Red Chimney Bar-B-Q	B	885-8744	817 N Canal St, Carlsbad	http:// www.redchimneybbq.com

A= American, B= Bar-B-Que, C= Chinese, D= Diner, G= Grill, H= Hotel, I= Italian, M=Mexican

Guadalupe Mountains

Name	Type	Phone (915)	Address	Website
Spanish Angels Cafe	M	964-2208	103 Main St, Dell, TX	None

A= American, B= Bar-B-Que, C= Chinese, D= Diner, G= Grill, H= Hotel, I= Italian, M=Mexican

13 TRANSPORTATION

The closest major airport is El Paso International Airport (ELP) and is approximately 65 miles from Guadalupe Mountains National Park.

http://www.elpasointernationalairport.com

Airlines

Airline	Connecting to	Phone	Website
Allegiant	Las Vegas, San Diego and seasonal to Orland/Sanford	(702) 505-8888	https://www.allegiantair.com
American Airlines	Dallas/Ft. Worth, Chicago, and Los Angeles	800 433-7300	https:// www.americanairlines.com/ homePage.do?locale=en_US
Delta	Atlanta	800 221-1212	https://www.delta.com/ home/
Frontier	Denver, Chicago	801 401-9000	https://www.flyfrontier.com
Southwest	Dallas Love Field, Houston, Las Vegas, Phoenix, San Antonio Austin, Los Angeles	800 435-9792	https://www.southwest.com
United	Denver, Houston	800 864-8331	https://www.united.com/ ual/en/us/

Car Rentals

	Reserve	Website
Advantage Rent A Car	800 777-5500	https:// www.advantage.com
Alamo	800 222-9058	https:// www.alamo.com/ en_US/car-rental/ home.html
Avis	800 230-4898	https:// www.avis.com/en/ home

	Reserve	Website
Budget	800-527-0700	https://www.budget.com/en/home
Dollar	800 800-4000	https://www.dollar.com
Enterprise	800 261-7331	https://www.enterprise.com/en/home.html
Hertz	800 654-3131	https://www.hertz.com/rentacar/reservation/
National	800 222-9058	https://www.nationalcar.com/en_US/car-rental/home.html
Payless	800 729-5377	https://www.paylesscar.com/en/home
Thrifty	800 847-4389	https://www.thrifty.com

14 OTHER NATIONAL UNITS IN THE AREA

Bureau of Land Management (BLM) https://www.blm.gov/visit/black-river-recreation-area	A 1,200 acre recreational area. They also have the La Cueva Non-Motorized Trail System that offers 2.200 acres, with 15 miles of maintained trails for mountain bikers, hiking, and equestrians. Along the river, you will find plants, fish, and reptiles.
White Sands National Monument https://www.nps.gov/whsa/index.htm	Rising from the heart of the Tularosa Basin is one of the world's great natural wonders - the glistening white sands of New Mexico. Great wave-like dunes of gypsum sand have engulfed 275 square miles of desert, creating the world's largest gypsum dunefield. White Sands National Monument preserves a major portion of this unique dunefield, along with the plants and animals that live here.

ISBN-10: - 1-946490-20-2
ISBN-13: - 978-1-946490-20-9

Made in United States
Orlando, FL
23 May 2022

18127299R00033